This book belongs to my Hero and Little Bee_____

who was diagnosed with _____ on this date _____ and

who Beat the Beast on this date_____

Picture of My Hero/Little Bee:

The Bug Who Thought He Lost His Buzz

What Happens When the Big Bad Beast Stings

by Kristen Barnett
pictures by Cindy Calzada

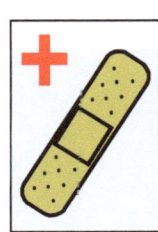

Text and illustrations © by Kristen Barnett and Cindy Calzada

All rights reserved. No part of this book may be reproduced in any form or by any electronic or mechanical means including information storage and retrieval systems - except in the case of brief quotations embodied in critical articles or reviews - without permission in writing.

The characters and events portrayed in this book are fictitious or are used fictitiously. Any similarity to real persons, living or dead, is purely coincidental and not intended by the author.

Keeping Faith Through Real Life

Watts Bugging You? Series:

At Watts Bugging You, we have a **BUG** mission to touch children's and parent's lives. Our series of children's books and products are aimed at helping parents talk through real life scenarios (eg. terminal illness, adoption, moving, divorce, disabilities, etc.) with their young children (2-7 yrs. old) using faith messages, children's language, and children's characters (Bugs).

As part of our mission to give back and support the families we serve, we are committed to donating a percentage of all book proceeds to organizations paying it forward to kids. If you are interested in partnering with us on our **BUG** mission, we'd love to hear from you! We're open to partnering with sponsors and endorsers who share our passion to reach the families who need to hear our messages the most. To reach us, you can contact Kristen Barnett, Author, at **kristen.barnett@wattsbuggingyou.com.**

To find out more about the series, please visit our website at **www.wattsbuggingyou.com.**

Watt's the Buzz.....

Dear Families,

"The Bug Who Thought He Lost His Buzz - What Happens When the Big, Bad Beast Stings" is near and dear to my heart due to all of the years I volunteered at Children's Hospital Colorado. While building strong relationships with families surviving their children's cancer treatments, I heard several families struggle with the same question..." Do I tell my young child they have Cancer and if yes how do I tell them?" This book introduces the topic of terminal illness using children's language, age appropriate topics, and characters (Bugs). It is also a tool for parents/caretakers to start conversations and to keep the door open for further discussions. Wherever you are in your treatment cycle or faith journey, this book is meant to add support to you and your family.

Again, my heart is with all families coping through this unimaginable challenge. I know it is not something you expected, but also know there is hope and there can be light at the end of the tunnel. For further support, please refer to our website community at **www.wattsbuggingyou.com**. We'd love to share stories and resources with you and hear your questions, personal story, and how we can further support you through your faith walk and healing journey.

Yours Truly, *Kristen C Burnett*

Dedication

This book I am dedicating to four angels whose spirit I believe are in every word of this book. First is my childhood friend, **Argie**, who at a young age had to witness her mother's battle with cancer. Poetry became her voice and with every word she had to cope with what no child should have to cope with; which is a love so big and a fear so unknown. It is due to my friend **Argie** I've become a writer. She gave me the gift of words.

Then there is the little boy, **Joshua**, in the hospital who clapped every time I entered his room and who loved to fall on his bed and laugh doing the chicken dance. His parents were the first to ask me – do I tell him he has Cancer? It is this little boy's spirit and his family's essence which gave my words purpose.

Next is **Brandan** who was not expected to beat the beast, but he did. Not only did he have a rare form of cancer, but he was allergic to majority of the medications. With God's hands, he became a survivor. It is **Brandan's** story that put the gift of faith into my words.

Last, but not least is **Christian**. Love this boy's name, but especially love his strength. As he endured heart complications at birth, liver cancer, and liver transplants all before he was five years old – he never gave up and never stopped fighting the beast. For years I put my dreams of writing aside, but it is **Christian's** endurance and positive outlook which have made my words come to life.

So for the four of you and many other families at Children's Hospital Colorado who had a huge impact on this book and the Watts Bugging You series – I want to thank you for every family who reads this book and who finds love and true meaning behind the words.

Finding Watts

In every book of the **Watts Bugging You Series**, you will find Watts hidden in each page of the story. Search and you will find him. This lovable firefly is there to follow you from the beginning to the end of your story. At times you'll easily find Watts and other times it may be more difficult, but if you follow his light you will eventually find him. You will find him in the good times and you will find him in the bad times. The good part is he'll always be there no matter "**Watt is Bugging You**".

So he zipped to a **beehive** full of **bandages**, nurses, and poles -

Where there were lots of other bees and lots of other colds.

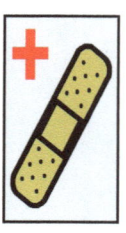  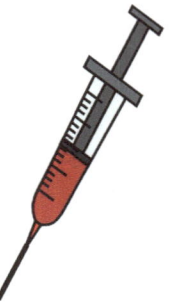

②

What happened, Doc, I am not myself today -

Can you please explain why my buzz has gone away?

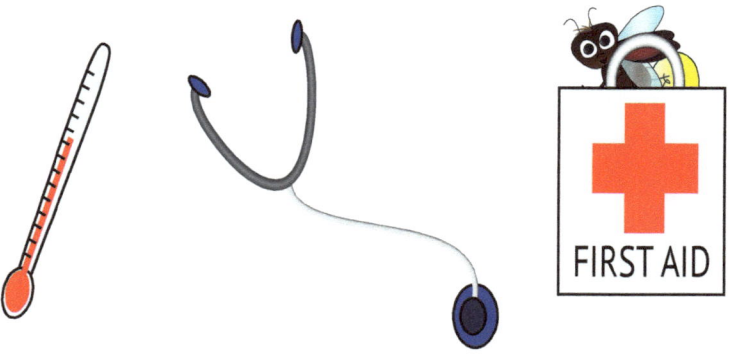

Doc Fuzz examined Bugsy from **antennae** to **wing**,

And said the Big, Bad **Beast** had stung his terrible **sting**.

Why can't this **beast** pick on someone his own size...

Why does he pick on us bumblebees, ladybugs, and flies?

Who is this **beast** who has shown his terrible **claws**?

Doesn't he know bugs hate the **boos**, **blues**, and blahs?

God **huffed** and he **puffed** and he said my son -

Don't give up when there is still a **battle** to be won.

But God, I have a **limp** in my step...

I have a **bruise** on my **wing**...

How can I possibly fight this thing?

God replied, do you think you're **alone**?

Don't you know I'm your **shield**, I'm your stone?

Nurses and doctors keep stopping by my room -

'When all I want is to go home right now, really **soon**.

Bugsy, this **beast** is bigger and badder than anyone knows -

Rely on your **faith** through both the highs and lows.

My beautiful bug, don't forget to **pray** and **believe** -

Believe my **grace** will never, ever, ever leave.

Yes, it is a tough road ahead - no one can disagree,

But we will fight hard against this bugly, ugly enemy.

My **peace** will carry you up, up, and away,

And our stingers will keep the **enemy** at bay.

We will zip and zap through every poke and prod -

We will **stare** at this **beast** with a **wink** and a **nod**.

Yes little bug, I hear every prayer, **cry**, and **tear** -

There is no reason to have an **ounce** of **fear**.

"But God what if I want to zip under this rock and hide?
   Will you still remain by my side?"

Or what if my **doubts** are bigger than the sky above?

Will you still want to show me your love?

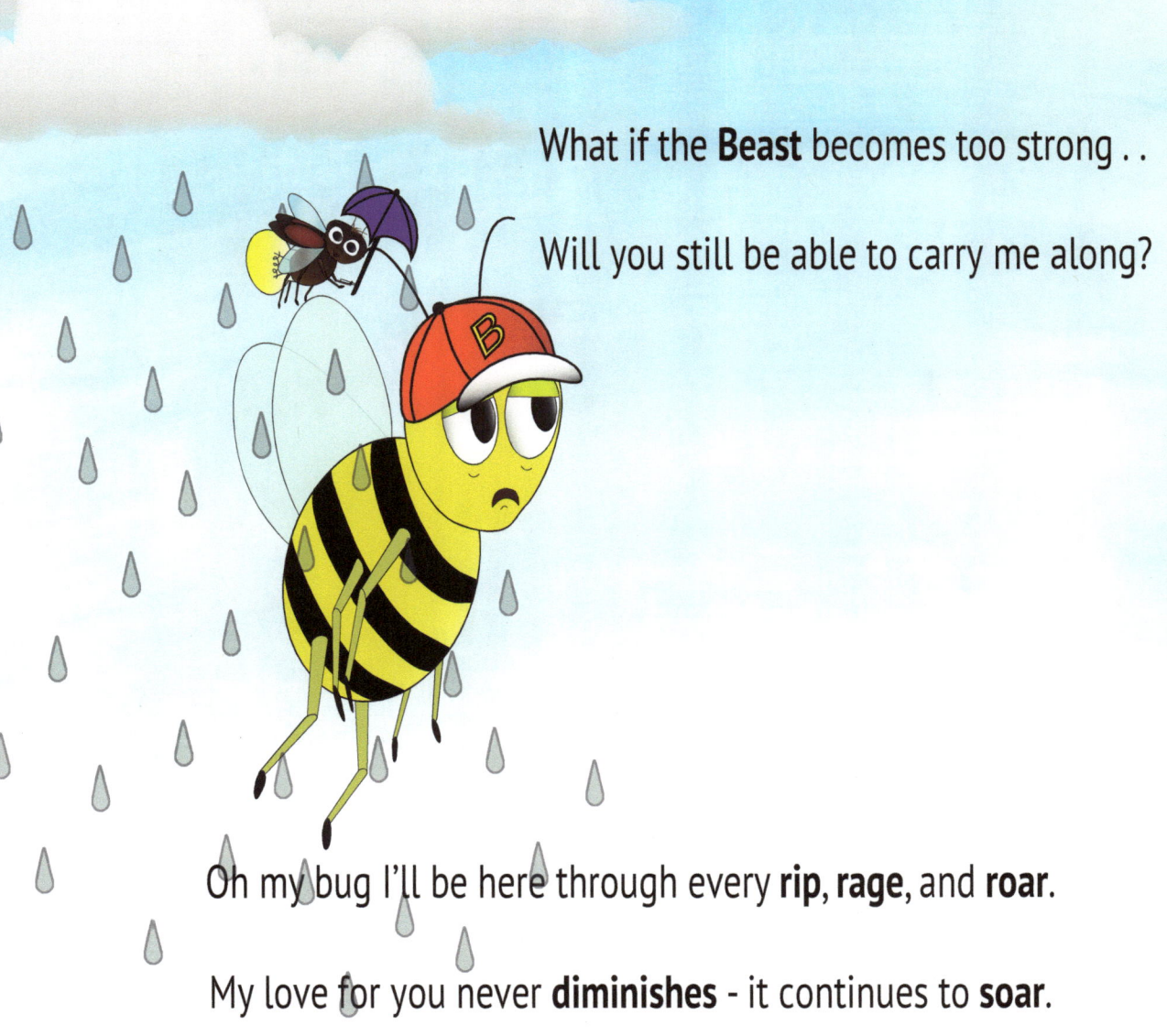

What if the **Beast** becomes too strong..

Will you still be able to carry me along?

Oh my bug I'll be here through every **rip**, **rage**, and **roar**.

My love for you never **diminishes** - it continues to **soar**.

I'll be here when you feel **yicky**, **yucky**, and rather sickly.

I'll be here when the pain has not gone away.

I'll be here when you **wonder** why again today.

I love you my Bug, I really, really, really do -

No matter what **believe** in yourself and **believe** in me too!

The story could have a different ending than you've **planned**,

But I've never stopped being your number one **fan**.

God - I've heard your words...

I've heard your heart,

But it's tough being **brave** and doing my part.

Sometimes I just want to scream really, really loud -

Or go hide myself within a big, poufy cloud.

But if I put on my big boy **wings** and know you are here...

Together we can fight this **battle** and fight my **fear.**

So please take my hand and give me your **strength** and **grace**

To **swish**, **swoosh** and put this Big, Bad **Beast** in his place!

Buzz Words....(Words highlighted and found in the book)

Alone – Being all by yourself
Antennae – Feelers on top of a bug's head
Bandages – Cloth that protects a cut
Battle – A fight until someone wins
Beast – A monster
Beehive – A bee's house shared with other bees
Believe – To know something is true
Boos, Blues, and Blahs – Feeling words for when someone is sad
Brave – Not afraid of a scary situation
Bruise – A black and blue mark which happens after bumping something
Claws – Sharp finger and toe nails on an animal's or beast's hands and feet
Continue – To keep doing something in the same way as you did it before
Cry and Tear – Being sad and having water fall from your eyes
Diminish – Getting smaller
Dive, Jazz, and Jive – They are all movements. Dive means to start up in the sky and jump to the ground using your hands first. Jazz and Jive are both dance movements, but Jazz is fast and slow movements and Jive is all fast movements.
Doubts – Not sure about something
Enemy – Someone or something bad you don't like
Faith – Trust in someone or something. It also means you think Jesus and God are true.
Fan – Excited friend or admirer
Fear – Being really scared
Grace – Good and kind things from God
Grouchy and Grumpy – A person who is unhappy and complains a lot

Huff and Puff – Sounds made when angry or frustrated. They sound like blowing slowly and loudly like what the big bad wolf did to the little pig's house.

Limp – Walking uneven after they get hurt and cannot stand on their foot

Medicine – A pill, liquid, or potion given by a Doctor to cure or treat sickness or an injury

Nod and Wink – An up and down shaking of the head and quick opening and closing of an eye

Ounce – A small part of something big

Pain – The feeling when your body hurts

Peace – Time of comfort

Poke and Prod - To push with your finger or another object

Planned – A set group of tasks or things to do

Pray – A way to speak to God

Reason - The right way to feel, act, or behave

Remain - To stay around even when others leave or to still have things to finish

Rip, Rage, and Roar - Words used to show or explain difficulty

Sigh and Snort – Sounds made when angry or frustrated. A sigh sounds like a big breath letting out while a snort sounds like a pig's sound.

Shield – A piece of metal a soldier holds in front of them to keep them safe when fighting

Soar – Go up, up, up like birds usually in the sky

Soon – Happening shortly

Stare – To look at one thing or person for a long time with your eyes open

Sting - A sharp object that is part of a bug's body used to poke people or animals when they feel they are in danger. A sting is also what you feel after the bug pokes you.

Strength – Very strong

Swish and Swoosh – Words used to describe moving forward and not giving up

Wing – Part of a bug's body which helps them fly

Wonder – The feeling when you are surprised or amazed at what you see or think

Yicky and Yucky – Words used to describe how you feel when you feel bad and sick

(BIBLE VERSES REFERRED TO IN THE BOOK)

Page 5: LET HIS LIGHT SHINE – 2 Cor 4:6
Page 10: HAVE FAITH IN GOD – 1 John 5:4
Page 14: DO NOT FEAR. GOD IS WITH YOU. – Deut 31:6

Buzz Time....(Reference and Support Tools):

On the **www.wattsbuggingyou.com** site there are support materials, questions, and conversation starters to continue discussing topics within the **"The Bug Who Thought He Lost His Buzz - What Happens When the Big, Bad Beast Stings."** Please note: The list may not be a comprehensive list of support materials, but is a starter kit derived of materials from my own experiences or shared knowledge. Although the Watts Bugging You Team recommends a few outside sites, we are not responsible for sentiments and information contained within the sites. Also, please contact your medical provider to provide additional resources available in your location.

* Resource Groups
* Questions to Ask Your Child
* Common Questions Your Child May Ask
* Discussion Topics for Your Sick Child and for their Siblings
* Activities for Families to Try
* Bible Verses and Prayer Examples by Topic Area
* Bible Stories to Read and Discuss With Your Family

Watts Bugging You Team:

Kristen Barnett (Author):

Kristen has a Bachelor's Degree in Creative Writing and Master's Degrees in both Counseling Psychology and Human Resource Development, is President at a management consulting firm called Evolve Consulting Group, but it is her experience with her faith journey, her 5 year old daughter, and volunteer work with young children living life's bumps and bruises that makes her the perfect author for her ministry and books. Like many of you, she asked the tough questions when she lost her daughter Hope, when she sat with parents who feared losing their young child to cancer, and when she wondered whether the adoption process would ever end. She listened and coached parents who didn't know what to say when life seemed bigger than them. It is these real life experiences which have led her to writing, healing, and not losing faith even when it was tough to see light at the end of the tunnel. Currently, Kristen lives in Colorado with her husband Phil, her daughter Ryley, and her dog Mugsy. She feels blessed to write the **Watts Bugging You Series** and prays her heart will shine through her words and will reach the hearts of the young angels and parents who need to hear the messages the most.

Cindy Calzada (Illustrator):

Cindy's journey as an artist began with being accepted into the Bollman art program in high school. There she mastered in classes such as 3D animation, photography, sculpting, painting, and metal shop. Continuing her education at Arizona State University taking art history classes, Cindy says it has been a tremendous journey and learning experience for her to work with different mediums and to perfect her craft. She believes it is with God's grace her creative journey has included such blessings as receiving a Commander's numbered coin award for a mural she painted on one of the air craft training hangers. As for the **Watts Bugging You Series,** Cindy is excited to work with the combination of water colors and computer generated art, but is also proud to be part of a project that can truly touch lives. Through life's hurdles of being a military wife and surviving several of her husband's deployments, to raising three sons, and marrying a man who was not raised with his faith Cindy has learned faith has kept her relationship strong and God's grace has made her dreams of being an illustrator come true. Now through her paintings and innate ability to make bugs come to to life, Cindy provides other families the important messages of faith, grace, and blessings. Currently Cindy with her husband, Aaron, and her three sons Darian, Andrew, and Timothy live on a military base in New Mexico, but will soon be transferring to a military base in Germany.

We'd Love to Hear From You:

Do you want to....
- Share your own story?
- Send us the picture of your little/bee hero that we can add to our site?
- Provide us feedback?
- Gain support through our blog or online community?
- Have us come talk at an event at your school, church, medical facility, or other event?
- Hear how we are paying it forward? Share how you are paying it forward?
- Buy additional copies of the **"Bug Who Thought He Lost His Buzz – What Happens When the Big, Bad Beast Stings"**, see what additional books are available in the series, or buy other products?
- Tell us about new book ideas?
- Ask us questions?
- Get involved with the **Watts Bugging You** mission and vision?

We are always looking for support, community, and the voice of our readers. We have a **Bug** mission to reach the parents and young children at the right time who are impacted by the topics within the **"Watts Bugging You"** series. To find out how you can assist us in spreading the word, sharing your own story, or to join in the **Watts Bugging You** community, please visit the **"Watts Bugging You"** site at: **www.wattsbuggingyou.com**.

www.ingramcontent.com/pod-product-compliance
Lightning Source LLC
Chambersburg PA
CBHW060822090426
42738CB00002B/74